Leader's Guide

by Mary Ellen Loren, I.H.M.

for

Meeting the Forgiving Jesus

A Child's Book for First Penance

One Liguori Drive
Liguori, Missouri 63057
(314) 464-2500

Imprimi Potest:
John F. Dowd, C.SS.R.
Provincial, St. Louis Province
Redemptorist Fathers

Imprimatur:
+ Edward J. O'Donnell
Vicar General, Archdiocese of St. Louis

ISBN 0-89243-225-X

Contents

To my Mom and Dad
To all who have helped me
meet the Forgiving Jesus
through the years
And especially to Nana
who prayed me
through this project.

About This Guide . . .

The lesson plans in this book show the fine touch of a religious educator who knows how to teach little children, and who understands the crucial need for forgiveness and healing in a world that is rent with divisions.

In addition to its content portions, each lesson plan offers suggestions for a prayerful celebration, enhancing the children's natural sense of liturgy.

Finally, and importantly, each lesson plan offers "Homework" suggestions, giving parents beautiful opportunities to share in their child's sacramental preparation. As the Greeley-Rossi report demonstrated years ago, "relatively little is accomplished by formal education . . . if the way is not prepared by the family environment." In light of that finding, the long-term effectiveness of this sacrament preparation program may depend on the link between home and school more than on any other measurable factor.

— The editor

ONE: HOW DO I SHOW LOVE?

1 When does God love me? God loves me all the time.

***Meeting the Forgiving Jesus,* page 8.**

Objective

To realize that God loves me all the time.

Materials Needed

- Various objects to be hidden in the classroom.
- Song: "Come Out" from the *Come Out* album by Jack Miffleton.
- Book: *When God Speaks* by Joan Lowery Nixon (Our Sunday Visitor, 1978).
- A piece of construction paper for each child.
- A magazine for each child.
- Scissors for all.
- Glue or paste for all.
- Filmstrip: *The Rock* from the God Is Like series (Ave Maria Press).
- Optional book: *God Is Like: Three Parables for Little Children,* Julie Walters (Ave Maria Press).
- Song: "All the Time" from the album *Bloom Where You Are Planted* by Carey Landry.
- A Bible.
- Song: "Our God Is a God of Love" from the *Hi God II* album by Carey Landry.
- A copy of a sheet of paper with the words I KNOW GOD LOVES ME for each child.

(*Note:* Religious music albums listed in this Guide, such as those by Carey Landry, Jack Miffleton, are available from Universal Publications/North American Liturgy Resources, 10802 North 23rd Avenue, Phoenix, AZ 85029.)

Experiences

Note: Before class, hide objects which the children will later find.

1. Ask:

Who knows what a detective is?

Say:

I wonder how many of you are good detectives. There are certain things which I have hidden in the room. First, I will describe what I have hidden. Then, everyone will have a chance to look for it. After each object is found, sit down and listen for the next clue.

(Substitute and/or add other objects to be found.) For example, add and say:

Look for something yellow that you can eat. (A banana)

Look for something round that bounces and is fun to play with. (A ball)

Look for something that is wet and white. You put it on cereal. (A carton of milk)

2. Introduce the song "Come Out." Say:

Listen for clues in this song that will tell you who you are looking for now.

Play the song "Come Out." Then ask:

Who are you looking for? (God) **What were some of the clues that helped you know the answer?**

3. Teach:

Even though we cannot see God, He is always with us, loving and taking care of us. All we have to do is follow the clues He gives us to find Him.

4. Read and discuss the story *When God Speaks* by Joan Lowery Nixon.

5. Ask:

Where do you think God is? (List the children's responses on the board.)

6. Give each child a piece of construction paper and a magazine. Tell the children to fold their paper into four squares. Explain that they are to find four different pictures in their magazines that show where God could be with them. Then they are to cut out and paste the pictures on their papers.

7. Read to the children the first two paragraphs on page 8 of *Meeting the Forgiving Jesus.* Lead them to realize that God is everywhere; that He is loving us all the time.

Celebration

— **Show the filmstrip** *The Rock.* (As an alternative, read the book *God Is Like,* by Julie Walters.)

Summarize:

Like the rock, God is always there. Like the rock, His love for us is strong.

— Have the children sit in a circle. Ask them to close their eyes and think for a moment about the times and places they feel close to God, times and places they feel God's love in a special way.

During this time play the song "All the Time."

— Say:

Jesus is the greatest sign of God's love for us. Jesus knows how much His Father loves us. Listen to this story Jesus once told about God.

Read Luke 12:22-32 (Do not be afraid; God cares for us).

— Lead the children in prayer:

Leader: In the Bible, God tells us:
"No matter what happens, I will always love you. . . . You are precious to me."
Class: Thank You, God, for loving me.
Leader: God loves us all so much that He gave us His only Son, Jesus.
Class: Thank You, God, for loving me.

— Close with the song "Our God Is a God of Love."

Homework

Give each child an I KNOW GOD LOVES ME paper.

Tell the children to ask their parents how they, the parents, know God loves them. The parents are to print *their* responses on the homework paper.

Remind the children that these homework papers will be shared in class.

2 How do I show God that I love Him? I pray. I take part in the Mass.

***Meeting the Forgiving Jesus*, page 9.**

Objective

To learn that I show God that I love Him when I pray and take part in the Mass.

Materials Needed

- Song "Smile" from the album *Bloom Where You Are Planted* by Carey Landry.
- Book: *That's What Friends Are For* by Florence Parry Heide and Sylvia Worth Van Clief (Four Winds Press, 1970).
- Optional filmstrip: *Growing in Awareness* (Thomas S. Klise Co.)
- Filmstrip: *Celebrating: A Special Way of Remembering* from the Our Church series (Winston House).
- Five pieces of colored construction paper for each child.
- A colored art chalk for each child.
- A stapler.
- A Bible.
- A loaf of unsliced bread.
- A pitcher of wine.
- Grape juice.
- Paper cups.
- Song: "Communion Medley" from the album *Bloom Where You Are Planted* by Carey Landry.
- A copy of the MY FAMILY PRAYS paper for each child (see page 14 of this Guide).

Experiences

1. Play the song "Smile."
Ask:
How many of you have friends who care for you? What is a friend?

2. Read and discuss the story *That's What Friends Are For.* Say:

The other animals gave advice and help to the elephant to show they were his friends. What else do you think friends can do to care for each other?

3. Introduce the children to the meaning of prayer as talking to God. Say:

One way to show we want to be someone's friend is to talk with them. We might say "Thank you," "Help me," "I'm sorry," or "I think you are great to a friend."

Demonstrate situations in which we might say these things.

4. Print the word PRAY on the board. Ask:

When we pray, who are we talking to? (God)

5. Help the children to understand that the same things we might say to a friend we also say to God when we pray. For example:

Thank you — prayer of thanksgiving.
Help me — prayer of petition.
I am sorry — prayer of sorrow.
I think you are great — prayer of praise.

6. Show the filmstrip *Growing in Awareness,* to reinforce the children's understanding of prayer.

7. Ask the children for examples of when they might say the different kinds of prayer described. Emphasize that we can pray anytime, anywhere.

8. Teach:

The Mass is a very special time to pray, to show God that we love Him, and to celebrate His love for us.

9. View and discuss the filmstrip *Celebrating: A Special Way of Remembering.*

10. Read the third paragraph on page 9 of *Meeting the Forgiving Jesus* to the children. Discuss how going to Mass shows God that we love Him.

11. Have the children make booklets based on page 9 of *Meeting the Forgiving Jesus.*

Let each child choose *four* different pieces of *colored* construction paper.

Give each child pieces of colored art chalk.

Put the following numbers and sentences on the board, one by one:

1. I GO TO MASS.
2. I LISTEN TO GOD'S WORD.
3. I PRAY AND SING.
4. I RECEIVE JESUS.

Have the children copy each sentence on their separate sheets of paper, leaving space for a picture.

Tell the children to draw a picture for each sentence.

Give each child a *white* piece of construction paper when they have all finished drawing their pictures on their first four pieces.

Draw a large square on the board. Print I SHOW GOD I LOVE HIM in the middle of the square. Tell the children to do the same on their white paper. Have them put their name on the bottom of the page.

Say:

Now, we are going to put our pictures into a booklet. This page will be the cover for your booklet. You may decorate it any way you wish.

Help assemble and staple the children's booklets together as they complete them.

Celebration

— Ask the children to gather in a circle around a table placed in the middle of the room. On the table have a Bible, a loaf of unsliced bread on a plate, and a pitcher of wine.

— Hold up the Bible. Say:

We show God that we love Him when we listen to His Word in the Bible.

— Read John 6:1-11 (the Feeding of the Five Thousand).

— Ask the children to sit down. Say:

The boy in the story knew how to be a friend. He shared what he had with others.

Hold up an unsliced loaf of bread on a plate and a pitcher of wine. Say:

Jesus shares Himself with us in Holy Communion as bread and wine.

Break off a piece of bread from the loaf for each child. Say:

Now, as friends, let us share what we have with each other.

Give the plate of bread to the child closest to you.

Tell the children they are to take a piece of bread and offer the plate to the person sitting next to them, saying I WANT TO BE YOUR FRIEND as they do so.

Have the children eat their piece of bread, once they have passed the plate.

Serve the children grape juice after they have shared and eaten their bread.

— Play the song "Communion Medley" as the children are sharing juice together.

Homework

— Give each child a MY FAMILY PRAYS paper. (On an 8½ x 11 sheet of paper, type the following headings. Leave space after headings for the family to write.)

MY FAMILY PRAYS
(Write a prayer for each heading.)
THANK YOU, GOD . . .
WE ARE SORRY, GOD . . .
PLEASE HELP US, GOD . . .
WE THINK YOU ARE GREAT, GOD . . .

— Tell the children to ask their parents to help them write a prayer they might say for each sentence on the paper.

— Remind the children to show their booklets and read page 9 of *Meeting the Forgiving Jesus* with their parents, to review the lesson.

3 How do I show God that I love myself? I care for myself. I learn. I play and work.

***Meeting the Forgiving Jesus,* page 10-11.**

Objective

To discover ways to show God that I love myself.

Materials Needed

- A large gift-wrapped box containing examples of creation.
- Filmstrip: *Creation: Why Is There an Outside?* from the Children of Light series (ROA's Films).
- Song: "All Your Gifts of Life" from the *Hi God II* album by Carey Landry.
- A piece of clay for each child.
- A piece of cardboard for each child.
- A large sheet of poster paper.
- Story: *Eight Bags of Gold* by Janice Kramer (Arch Book, Concordia Press).
- Film: *A Talent for Tony* (Teleketics).
- Song: "If I Were a Butterfly" from the *Hi God II* album by Carey Landry.
- A "THANKS, GOD" paper for each child.

Experiences

1. Display a large gift-wrapped box with a tag labeled, TO MY CHILDREN WITH LOVE, attached to it. Ask the children to guess what might be in the box.

2. Open the box. Show different wonders of creation in the box — e.g., a flower, a plant, a rock, a goldfish, etc. Ask:
Who do you think made all these gifts?

3. View and discuss the filmstrip *Creation: Why Is There an Outside?*

4. Listen to the song "All Your Gifts of Life." Give, ask for other examples of God's creation for which we should be thankful.

5. Give each child a piece of clay and a piece of cardboard. Tell the children to "create" one of their favorite gifts in God's world from the clay.

6. Have each child share his or her creation and then put it on display.

7. Teach:

Of all the wonderful things God has created and loves, God loves us the best. God wants us to love ourselves as much as He does.

8. Show the children a large poster with the words I SHOW GOD THAT I LOVE MYSELF WHEN . . .

9. Print I CARE FOR MYSELF on the poster. Ask for and list on the poster the children's examples of caring for themselves.

10. Print I LEARN on the poster. Ask for and list examples of learning.

11. Print I PLAY AND WORK on the poster. Ask for and list examples of playing and working.

12. Ask volunteers to role-play in silence various ways to care for ourselves, to learn, to play and work. Have the rest of the children guess what the example might be.

13. Read page 11 of *Meeting the Forgiving Jesus* for other examples of how we show God that we love ourselves.

Celebration

— Say:

God has given us many wonderful gifts in creation. He has also given each one of us a very special gift called a talent. A talent is anything we can do well.

— Share examples of different talents the children might think they have.

— Introduce the story of the Parable of the Talents. Say:
The story you are about to hear tells us that God thinks whatever talents He has given us are very important, no matter what they are. God also wants us to use our talents well.

— Read the book *Eight Bags of Gold,* which is about Matthew 25:14-30.

— View and discuss the film *A Talent for Tony.* Stress the important lesson that Tony learned: The most important talent Tony had was belief in himself.

— Sing "If I Were a Butterfly." Encourage the children to do spontaneous actions to the song while it is playing.

— Say the prayer on page 11 of *Meeting the Forgiving Jesus.*

Homework

Give each child a "THANKS, GOD" paper. Here is what it says at the top of the paper (the rest of the paper is blank):

THE ______________________________ FAMILY

THANKS, GOD, FOR . . .

Have the children print their last name on the designated line.
Tell the children they are to talk with their family about the wonderful gifts God has given them.
Explain that each member of the family is to write, draw, or cut out and paste a magazine picture of something in creation they want to thank God for on this homework paper. Underneath what they have written, drawn, or pasted, they write their first names.
Remind the children to read pages 10 and 11 of *Meeting the Forgiving Jesus* with their parents, to review the lesson.

4 How do I show God that I love others? I pray for others. I help others.

***Meeting the Forgiving Jesus,* pages 12-13.**

Objective

To discover that I show God I love others by praying for and helping them.

Materials Needed

- A large ball with the Scripture saying, LOVE ONE ANOTHER, printed on it.
- Song: "Giant Love Ball Song" from the *Hi God* album by Carey Landry.
- Story book: *Love Is a Special Way of Feeling* by Joan Walsh Anglund (Harcourt, 1960).
- Song: "The Good Samaritan" from the *Dandelions* album by Mary Lu Walker.
- Filmstrip: *Franklin* from The Parables, Primary II (Twenty-Third Publications).
- Song: "Happy the Heart" from the *Hi God* album by Carey Landry.
- A heart pattern for each child (Pattern 1 on page 40 of this Guide).
- A hole puncher.
- Pieces of yarn for each child.
- Song: "What Makes Love Grow" from the *Hi God* album by Carey Landry.
- A "Loving Tree" (tree branches potted in clay).
- "Loving Tree" paper (Pattern 2 on page 41 of this Guide).

Experiences

1. Have the children stand in a circle. Show them a large ball. Bounce the ball to one of the children and have him or her read what is printed on the ball: LOVE ONE ANOTHER. Ask:

What do you think this means?
Share ideas.

2. Introduce the "Giant Love Ball Song." Say:
As we listen to the "Giant Love Ball Song," bounce the ball to the person standing next to you in the circle.

3. Play the "Giant Love Ball Song." When all the children have had a turn bouncing the ball, ask them to sit down in a circle.

4. Say:
Today we are going to talk about love and find out how to love each other the way Jesus loves us.

5. Read and discuss the story, *Love Is a Special Way of Feeling,* by Joan Walsh Anglund.

6. Recall different stories of Jesus helping, loving others — e.g., curing the blind man (John 9:1-38 or Matthew 20:29-34), feeding the five thousand (John 6:1-15).

7. Listen to the song "The Good Samaritan" on the *Dandelions* album. Discuss how the song shows that Jesus wants us to help and love others.

8. Show the filmstrip *Franklin,* to emphasize Jesus' command to love one another.

9. Discuss and act out ways we, too, can be good Samaritans by helping at home, in school, etc.

10. Read and discuss page 12 and the first paragraph on page 13 of *Meeting the Forgiving Jesus.*

11. Pray spontaneously for other people whom the children wish to mention.

12. Say:
I also show God that I love others when I help them.

13. Read the second paragraph on page 13 of *Meeting the Forgiving Jesus.*

Celebration

— Play the song "Happy the Heart" from the *Hi God* album.

— Give each child a heart pattern (Pattern 1). Have the children cut it out, punch out the hole, and attach yarn to it.

— On the chalkboard print the words I PRAY FOR. . . . Have the children copy this on their paper hearts. Then have them write the name of someone they will pray for. (Suggest that they use page 13 of *Meeting the Forgiving Jesus* for their ideas.)

— On the chalkboard print the words I HELP OTHERS. . . . Have the children copy this on the other side of their paper hearts. Then have them write something they will do to help others.

— Show the children the "Loving Tree." (The children will hang their hearts on the tree branches potted in clay.)

— Say:

Every time we help or we pray for someone our love grows.

— Have the children place their hearts on the "Loving Tree" branches as they listen to the song "What Makes Love Grow."

— Together, say the prayer at the bottom of page 13 in *Meeting the Forgiving Jesus.*

Homework

— Give each child a copy of the "Loving Tree" paper (Pattern 2).

— Have the children talk with their families about ways they can show love for each other at home.

— Tell the children to write on the "Loving Tree" hearts what each member of their family is going to do to make love grow.

— Remind the children to bring the hearts back to the next class so that they can share what they wrote.

TWO: HOW DO I RECEIVE FORGIVENESS?

5 How do children sin? Children sin by being selfish on purpose.

***Meeting the Forgiving Jesus,* pages 14-15.**

Objective

To understand the difference between sin, accidents, and mistakes.

Materials Needed

- Filmstrip: *God Loves Us* from the Religious Awareness Filmstrips (Thomas S. Klise Co.).
- Two flash cards for each child labeled ACCIDENT and MISTAKE.
- A picture of an unhappy person.
- "Sad Sam" game (Pattern 3 on page 42 of this Guide).
- Song: "Sometimes It's Not Easy" from the *Hurray for God* album by Lou Fortunate (Sadlier).
- Record and book: *The Dirty Devil and the Carpenter's Boy* The Purple Puzzle Tree (Concordia Publishing House).
- "Sad Sam" paper (Pattern 4 on page 43 of this Guide).

Experiences

1. Introduce the filmstrip *God Loves Us.* Ask:

   Have you ever had an accident? Have you ever made a mistake? Were people upset with you? How did you feel?

   Share experiences.

Say:

Today we are going to see a filmstrip that shows how God loves us even when we make mistakes or have accidents.

2. View and discuss the filmstrip.

3. Give each child two flash cards — one labeled ACCIDENT and the other labeled MISTAKE. Explain that accidents and mistakes are actions not done deliberately, not done on purpose.

4. Point out that nobody is perfect. Have the children write or draw a "Nobody's Perfect" story on the back of each flash card, giving an example of an accident they may have had or a mistake they might have made.

5. Ask volunteers to tell their "Nobody's Perfect" stories. After each story have the rest of the children hold up the appropriate flash card that describes what kind of an action it was: accident or mistake.

6. Read page 14 of *Meeting the Forgiving Jesus* to reinforce the children's understanding of accidents and mistakes.

7. Print the word *sin* on the board. Ask:

Does anyone know what this word means?

8. Explain the difference between sins, accidents, and mistakes. Say:

Accidents and mistakes I do not do on purpose. But when I sin, I know something is wrong to do, and I do it anyway. I choose to be selfish on purpose. I say no to God's love. I deliberately hurt someone or refuse to do something I am supposed to do.

9. Read and discuss page 15 of *Meeting the Forgiving Jesus* for examples of selfishness and sin. Have the children give their own examples of selfishness and sin as well — e.g., taking something that does not belong to them, not telling the truth, etc.

10. Introduce Sad Sam to the children.

Put a picture of an unhappy person on the board. Point to the picture and say:

This is Sad Sam. Sad Sam is a person just like you and me. Sad Sam is not perfect. Sometimes he forgets and makes mistakes. Sometimes he even hurts people on purpose. But Sad Sam also knows that God loves him anyway. He knows that God is always ready to help him try to be his best. All Sad Sam has to do is ask.

11. Present the "Sad Sam" game to review what sins, accidents, and mistakes are.

Give each child a "Sad Sam" game board (Pattern 3). Explain that each story on the board is either an example of a sin, an accident, or a mistake that Sad Sam has made.

Say:

After I read each story, print an "S" in the story's circle if you think it is a sin, an "A" if it is an accident, or an "M" if it is a mistake.

12. Read each story. Check and discuss the answers the children wrote. Make certain to clarify any misunderstanding between sin, accident, and mistake the children might have had.

Celebration

— Play the song "Sometimes It's Not Easy."

Say:

We know that it is not always easy to say yes to God's love. But we have Jesus to show us how to say yes, to do what God wants us to do.

— Listen to the story of *The Dirty Devil and the Carpenter's Boy* from The Purple Puzzle Tree (Matthew 4:1-11).

Say:

We, like Jesus, want to be what God asks us to be: His loving sons and daughters. Let us promise God that with His help we will try to say yes and love as Jesus loves.

— Pray the Promise Prayer on page 31 of *Meeting the Forgiving Jesus.*

Homework

— Tell the children to read and discuss pages 14 and 15 of *Meeting the Forgiving Jesus* with their parents, to review the lesson.

— Give each child a copy of the "Sad Sam" paper (Pattern 4). Have the children talk with their parents about times when they — the children — have been a Sad Sam, times when they have made mistakes, have had accidents, or have deliberately done something wrong at home. Acting as secretaries, the parents are to write the child's responses in the appropriate space.

— Ask the children to say the Promise Prayer at home with their parents.

6 How does God want me to forgive others? God wants me to forgive as He forgives me.

***Meeting the Forgiving Jesus,* page 16.**

Objective

To realize that God wants me to forgive others as He forgives me.

Materials Needed

- Problem situations on index cards.
- Book: *The Unforgiving Servant* by Janice Kramer (Arch Book, Concordia Publishing House).
- Song: "This Is My Commandment" from the album *Hi God II* by Carey Landry.
- A Bible.
- A Cross pattern (Pattern 5 on page 44 of this Guide).
- Scissors.
- Crayons.
- Song: "Peace Time" from the album *Hi God* by Carey Landry.
- Sheets of paper.

Experiences

1. Stage a mock argument.
(Before class, prearrange a shoving match between two students trying to be first in line. Have the shoving match develop into a verbal argument and finally a physical confrontation.)

2. Settle the argument. Then ask:
What do these children have to do to be friends again?

3. Read the first paragraph on page 16 of *Meeting the Forgiving Jesus* to the children.
Ask:
What would you do if you were David?

4. Continue with the second paragraph on page 16 of *Meeting the Forgiving Jesus,* to emphasize the need for a forgiving attitude.

5. Have the children give examples of situations when they have been hurt by something someone has done — e.g., name-calling, teasing, taking something that belongs to them.

6. Give volunteers index cards with problem situations printed on them. Examples would be:
— Two children wanting the same ball on the playground;
— A child talking back to parents;
— Children refusing to let another child join their game.
(The number of problem situations is up to the teacher.)

7. Ask the volunteers to role-play the situation for the entire class. After each role play, have the rest of the children give a possible solution to the problem, suggesting various signs of making up, of forgiveness.

8. Point out to the children that there were times in the life of Jesus when people, even His closest friends, hurt Him.

9. Tell the story of Peter's denial (Luke 22:54-62) in your own words.

Say:

Even though Peter hurt Jesus, still Jesus understood Peter's fear and his weakness, and Jesus looked at him with love and forgiveness.

10. Teach: God wants us to forgive as He forgives us.

11. Read the story of *The Unforgiving Servant* to reinforce how important it is to forgive.

12. Play the song "This Is My Commandment."

Celebration

— Begin with the Sign of the Cross.

Say:

The Cross is Jesus' sign of peace and forgiveness. Even as He was dying on the Cross, Jesus was willing to forgive those who hurt Him.

— Read Luke 23:33-34 to the children.

Say:

As a sign that we want to forgive as Jesus forgives, we are going to make our own peace cross.

— Give each child a pattern of a cross (Pattern 5). Tell the children to print the words JESUS FORGIVES on one side of the cross and the words I FORGIVE on the other side of the cross. After they have done this, have them decorate and cut out their crosses.

— Play the song "Peace Time."

— Together, say the prayer on page 16 of *Meeting the Forgiving Jesus.*

— Exchange the peace crosses as a sign of our willingness to forgive each other. Say the words JESUS FORGIVES, I FORGIVE as the crosses are exchanged.

— Close with this blessing:

Leader: "Be friends with one another, forgiving as God forgives you. In the name of the Father, and of the Son, and of the Holy Spirit."

Class: Amen.

Homework

— Pass out sheets of drawing paper, one to each child. Ask the children to fold their paper in half. Say:

Perhaps this week you have done something at home that made someone in your family unhappy. Talk with your family about this. On one half of the paper draw a picture of what happened. On the other half draw a happy ending to the story.

Encourage the children to say I'm sorry, to make up with anyone in their family they might have hurt through selfishness.

7 When does God forgive my sins? God forgives me when I am sorry for my sins. At Holy Mass I ask God to forgive me.

***Meeting the Forgiving Jesus,* page 17.**

Objective

To present the Mass as a special time to ask for and receive God's forgiveness.

Materials Needed

- Song: "What Shall I Do?" from the album *Hi God II* by Carey Landry.
- A Bible.
- A poster with the Our Father printed on it.
- A picture of people exchanging the Sign of Peace.
- Copies of the parts of Mass in which we seek God's forgiveness (the Penitential Rite, the Our Father, the Lamb of God) — one copy for each child.
- Book: *The Boy Who Ran Away* by Irene Elmer (Arch Book, Concordia Publishing House).
- Song: "Song of the Loving Father" from the album *Hi God II* by Carey Landry.
- Song: "Peace Is Flowing Like a River" from *Hi God II.*

Experiences

1. Listen to the song "What Shall I Do?"

2. Review situations in which we have to say "I'm sorry" — e.g., being unkind, being disobedient, etc.

3. Stress that God is always ready to forgive us when we are sorry.

4. Introduce and read the story of the Prodigal Son (Luke 15:12-20) to show God's readiness to forgive.

5. Have the children share experiences of people in their lives who have loved and forgiven them.

6. Present the Mass as a special time to ask for and receive God's forgiveness. Explain the Penitential Rite. Say:

At the beginning of Mass we remember our selfishness and sin. We ask for God's forgiveness when we pray "Lord, have mercy." This part of the Mass is called the Penitential Rite. (Write *"May Almighty God . . . forgive us our sins"* on the chalkboard.) **When Father says "May Almighty God . . . forgive us our sins," God knows we are sorry.**

7. Display a poster with the words to the Our Father. Say the Our Father together.

Point out that at Mass when we pray "Forgive us our trespasses as we forgive those who trespass against us," we are again telling God that we are sorry for our sins and willing to forgive others.

8. Show a picture of people exchanging the Sign of Peace at Mass. Explain that shaking hands at Mass is a sign that we want to forgive and be forgiven.

Demonstrate the Sign of Peace by doing it with several of the children, and teach the response for this part of the Mass: "Peace be with you. And also with you."

9. Recite the Lamb of God prayer for the children. Then say:

In this prayer we are asking Jesus, who takes away the sins of the world, to forgive our sins as well.

Now have the children say the Lamb of God prayer together.

10. Read together page 17 in *Meeting the Forgiving Jesus,* to review the parts of the Mass in which we ask God to forgive us.

Celebration

— Act out the story of the Prodigal Son, using the book *The Boy Who Ran Away.*

— Form a circle. Play "Song of the Loving Father."

— *Leader:* For the times we have been selfish and wanted our own way. Lord, have mercy.
Class: Lord, have mercy.

Leader: For the times we have said no to God's love. Christ, have mercy.
Class: Christ, have mercy.
Leader: For the times we have not loved as Jesus loves. Lord, have mercy.
Class: Lord, have mercy.
Leader: May Almighty God have mercy on us, forgive us our sins, and bring us to everlasting life.
Class: Amen.

— Play the song "Peace Is Flowing Like a River" as the children exchange a sign of peace.

— Join hands and pray the Our Father together.

Homework

— Give each child a copy of the following lineup of parts of the Mass that ask for God's forgiveness. Tell the children that their task is to match the right words with the right parts of the Mass. Here is the scrambled lineup:

PENITENTIAL RITE — PEACE BE WITH YOU.
AND ALSO WITH YOU.

OUR FATHER
LORD, HAVE MERCY.
MAY ALMIGHTY GOD . . .
FORGIVE US OUR SINS.

SIGN OF PEACE
LAMB OF GOD WHO TAKES AWAY THE SINS OF THE WORLD.

LAMB OF GOD
FORGIVE US OUR TRESPASSES AS WE FORGIVE THOSE WHO TRESPASS AGAINST US

On the back of the paper, have the children draw people at Mass giving each other the Sign of Peace.

— Have the children ask members of their family to say something they are sorry for, pray the Our Father, and share a Sign of Peace before eating together.

THREE: HOW DO I MEET JESUS IN PENANCE?

8 What is the Sacrament of Penance? Penance is Jesus' way of showing He forgives me.

***Meeting the Forgiving Jesus*, pages 18-19.**

Objective

To understand that the Sacrament of Penance is Jesus' way of showing He forgives me.

Materials Needed

- Drawing paper for each child.
- Pictures of a baptism and of someone taking part in the Sacrament of Penance.
- A chalice and some hosts.
- Book: *The Hating Book* by Charlotte Zolotow (Scholastic Book Services, 1969).
- The story of Zacchaeus ("The Man in the Tree") from *A Child's Bible/New Testament* (Paulist Press).
- Filmstrip: *Jesus, a Friend Forever* from Reconciliation and Penance (Twenty-Third Publications).
- Song: "Love One Another" from the album *Make a Wonderful Noise* by Jack Miffleton.
- Sad-Happy pattern (Pattern 6 on page 45 of this Guide).

Experiences

1. Pass out drawing paper. Have the children fold their paper into four squares. Ask them to draw a picture of themselves as a baby and as they are right now in the two top squares.

2. Show a picture of a baptism. Say:

When you were a baby, something special happened to you. Your parents took you to a priest. You were baptized.

3. Print the word BAPTISM on the board. Explain that Baptism gives us the new life of Jesus. It makes us members of Jesus' family.

4. Tell the children to draw a picture of Baptism under their baby picture and label the picture "Baptism."

5. Display a chalice and hosts used at Mass. Print the words HOLY COMMUNION on the board.

Say:

Now that you are older, you are getting ready to receive the Body and Blood of Jesus in Holy Communion. Jesus wants you to be His very special friend.

6. Have the children draw a picture of themselves receiving Holy Communion in the remaining square and print HOLY COMMUNION under the picture.

7. Point out to the children that Baptism and Holy Communion have a special name. Print the word SACRAMENT on the board.

8. Explain that sacraments are Jesus' signs of His special love for us. He gives us the sacraments of Baptism and Holy Communion to help us be His friends.

9. Remind the children that we do not always love as we should. We do not always act like friends of Jesus. Sometimes we are selfish. (Refer to page 15 of *Meeting the Forgiving Jesus.)*

10. Read *The Hating Book* by Charlotte Zolotow. Discuss how the characters in the story hurt their friendship; how they failed to love; how they eventually made up.

11. Teach the meaning of reconciliation (to forgive, to be friends again) in relation to the story in *The Hating Book.*

12. Ask the children to give similar examples of the need for reconciliation from their own experience.

13. Introduce the Sacrament of Penance (Reconciliation) as Jesus' way of showing He forgives and still loves us even when we do not love as we should.

14. Together, read and discuss page 19 in *Meeting the Forgiving Jesus.*

15. Show a picture of someone receiving the Sacrament of Penance.

Put the word PENANCE on the board.

Ask the children to print the word PENANCE on the back of their Baptism/Holy Communion drawings. Then have them draw a picture of themselves receiving this sacrament from the priest.

Celebration

— Read the story of Zacchaeus ("The Man in the Tree") from *A Child's Bible/New Testament.*

— Reflect prayerfully together on how we are like Zacchaeus.

— View the filmstrip *Jesus, a Friend Forever.*

— Play the song "Love One Another" by Jack Miffleton.

Homework

— Tell the children to take their sacrament paper home and teach their parents about Baptism, Holy Communion, and Penance.

— Give each child a Sad-Happy pattern (Pattern 6). Explain that on the Sad side they are to draw or write something they have done to make someone unhappy. On the other side they are to draw or write something they have done to make someone happy.

— Remind the children to ask their parents to read pages 18-19 in *Meeting the Forgiving Jesus* with them at home.

9 How do I get ready to celebrate Penance? I pray. I examine my life. I tell God I am sorry.

***Meeting the Forgiving Jesus,* pages 20-21.**

Objective

To get ready to celebrate Penance through an examination of conscience.

Materials Needed

- Some tiny seeds.
- A display table with some small objects on it.
- A few magnifying glasses.
- A poster with words to the song "Sometimes It's Not Easy."
- A copy of Examination of Conscience Questions (Pattern 7 on page 46 of this Guide) for each child.
- A copy of the Family Promise Paper (Pattern 8 on page 47 of this Guide) for each child.
- Song: "Sometimes It's Not Easy" from the album *Hurray for God* by Lou Fortunate (Sadlier).

Experiences

1. Hold one or more tiny seeds in your hand. Ask the children what could be used to make the seeds easier to look at, to examine. (The answer you want is: a magnifying glass.)

2. Give each child an opportunity to examine various small objects on a display table, using a magnifying glass. Ask for a few volunteers to describe what they see.

3. Recall the two great commandments of Jesus: *Love God. Love your neighbor.* Explain that today we are going to examine something that tells how well we are following these two commandments.

4. Print the word CONSCIENCE on the board. Say:

Our conscience helps us to know right from wrong. We can examine our conscience by looking at how we behave, how we act toward God, toward others.

5. Display the poster with the words to the song "Sometimes It's Not Easy." Listen to the song and discuss times and places when it's not easy to be good — e.g., at home, school, playground, church.

6. Give each child a copy of the Examination of Conscience Questions (Pattern 7) to help examine behavior. Use examples to clarify what each question means. Say:

These questions help us to examine our love for God, our love for ourselves, and our love for our neighbor.

I am going to read each question again. At the end of each question you will see a circle. After I have read the question, you are to draw a smile in the circle if your answer is yes. If your answer is no, you are to draw a frown.

Please do not fill in the circles until I read the question out loud. Before you fill in the circle, think carefully and BE HONEST!

Celebration

— After they have completed their examination papers, ask the children to listen very quietly as you pray the prayer on page 20 of *Meeting the Forgiving Jesus.*

— Tell the children to find those questions for which they have drawn a frown. Say:

Think about the times you have been selfish to God, to your family, to your friends. Ask yourself: Did I mean to do that? Did I do that on purpose?

— Ask volunteers to share something they are sorry for.

— Have the class respond with "Lord, have mercy."

— Pray the Our Father together.

Homework

— Have the children take their examination papers home and ask their parents to answer the questions themselves.

— Ask the children to talk with their parents about what they can do to be more loving as a family.

— Give each child a FAMILY PROMISE PAPER (Pattern 8).

— Explain that each family is to choose one thing they will do together to be more loving, write it on the Family Promise Paper, and return it to class.

— Turn to page 21 in *Meeting the Forgiving Jesus.* Tell the children to ask their parents to help them learn the prayers on this page.

10 How do I celebrate Penance with the priest? Father and I share the forgiveness of Jesus.

***Meeting the Forgiving Jesus*, pages 22-23.**

Objective

To learn how to celebrate the Sacrament of Penance with the priest.

Materials Needed

- A pencil.
- Mending materials — glue or tape.
- A flannel board.
- Flannel board signs for steps in the Rite of Penance.
- Copies of steps in the Rite of Penance (Pattern 9 on page 48 of this Guide).
- Scissors — enough for all.
- A business-size envelope for each child.
- Filmstrip: *Celebrating the Friendship of Jesus* from Reconciliation and Penance (Twenty-Third Publications).
- Song: "What Do I Do?" from the *Hi God II* album by Carey Landry.

Experiences

1. Break a pencil in front of the children. Discover and demonstrate ways the pencil could be mended and put back together.

2. Remember how the characters in *The Hating Book* (read in Lesson 8) hurt or broke their friendship.

3. Recall the meaning of the word *reconciliation:* to forgive, to be friends again. Discuss what the friends in the story did to reconcile their differences.

4. Review the Sacrament of Penance (Reconciliation) as a means of reconciliation with God, myself, and others. (See page 19 of *Meeting the Forgiving Jesus.*)

5. Present the way Penance is celebrated with the priest:

Have flannel board signs and corresponding pictures for each step in the Rite of Penance. Use the same words found on pages 22-23 of *Meeting the Forgiving Jesus.*

Place each step in the Rite of Penance, one by one, on the flannel board and explain it.

6. Play "Reconciliation Race."

Give each child a copy of the steps for the Rite of Penance (Pattern 9). Have the children cut out the sections along the dotted lines.

Mix up the Reconciliation steps on your flannel board. Tell the children to do the same with their own sets.

Explain the rules of the "Reconciliation Race." Say:

Now we are going to see who can put these signs on the flannel board in the correct order.

But first you must put your own set of signs in order.

When you have done so, race to the flannel board and straighten out that set. I will write your name on the chalkboard as you finish.

Before you go to your seat, please mix up the flannel board signs again.

You may help others finish the race once you have had a turn at the flannel board.

Caution the children to be careful. Say:

If you put the flannel board signs in the wrong order, you will only have to return to your place to try again. It's more important to take your time and run the race the right way than to finish fast.

The "race" goes on until everyone has had a chance at the flannel board.

Give each child a business-size envelope when everyone has finished. Tell the children to put their reconciliation steps in the envelope to take home.

7. Show the filmstrip *Celebrating the Friendship of Jesus* to review how to celebrate the Sacrament of Penance with the priest.

8. Role-play someone taking part in the Sacrament of Penance.

9. Take a tour of the confessionals (Reconciliation rooms) in church. Answer any questions children may have.

Celebration

— Sit in a circle.

— Listen to the song "What Do I Do?"

— Guide the children in an examination of conscience. Use the questions under the heading "Have I shown love for others?" on page 26 of *Meeting the Forgiving Jesus.*

— Say:

Close your eyes and silently tell Jesus you are sorry for the times you have hurt others by being selfish. Ask Jesus to forgive you.

— Say:

Share the Sign of Peace with the person next to you as a gesture of reconciliation.

Homework

— Refer to pages 22-23 in *Meeting the Forgiving Jesus.*

— Tell the children they are to ask their parents to read these two pages with them at home.

— Remind the children to take their envelopes home. Encourage them to play "Reconciliation Race" with their family.

Pattern 1
Lesson 4

HEART PATTERN

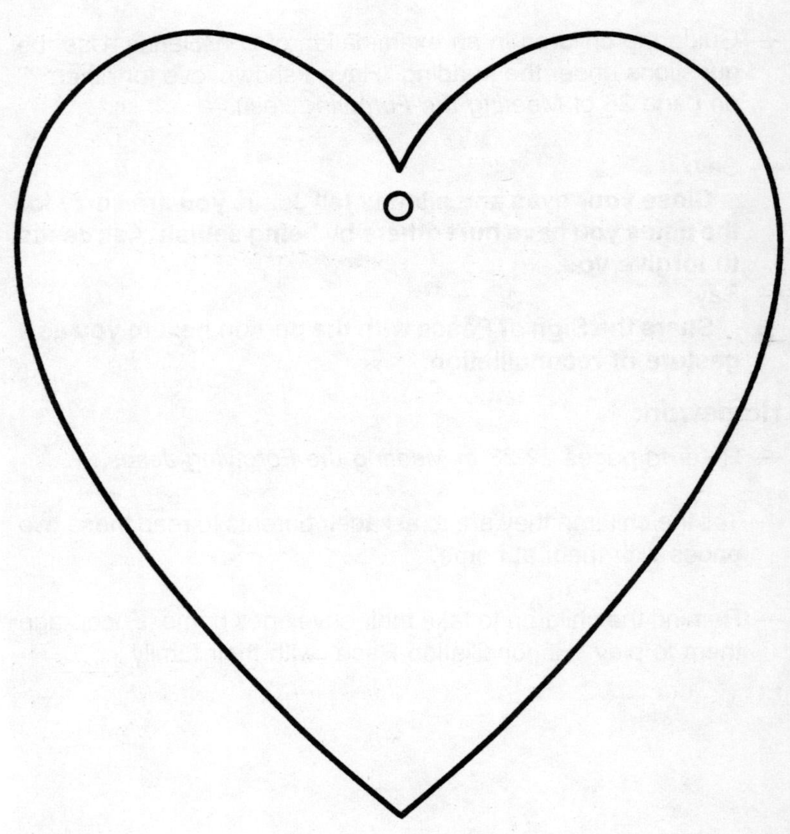

Pattern 2
Lesson 4

LOVING TREE PAPER

Pattern 3
Lesson 5

On his math paper Sad Sam adds two plus two. His answer is five.

Sad Sam forgets to hang up his clothes.

Sad Sam takes a candy bar from the store without paying for it.

Sad Sam breaks a window while playing baseball.

Sad Sam disobeys his parents and rides his bike in the street.

Sad Sam is angry at his little sister. He hits her.

Sad Sam does not say thank you when his friend gives him a pencil to use.

Running on the playground, Sad Sam does not watch where he is going. He bumps into someone and knocks them down.

Pattern 4
Lesson 5

I AM A SAD SAM WHEN I . . . **SIN**

I AM A SAD SAM WHEN I . . . **ACCIDENT**

I AM A SAD SAM WHEN I . . . **MISTAKE**

Pattern 5
Lesson 6

Cross Pattern

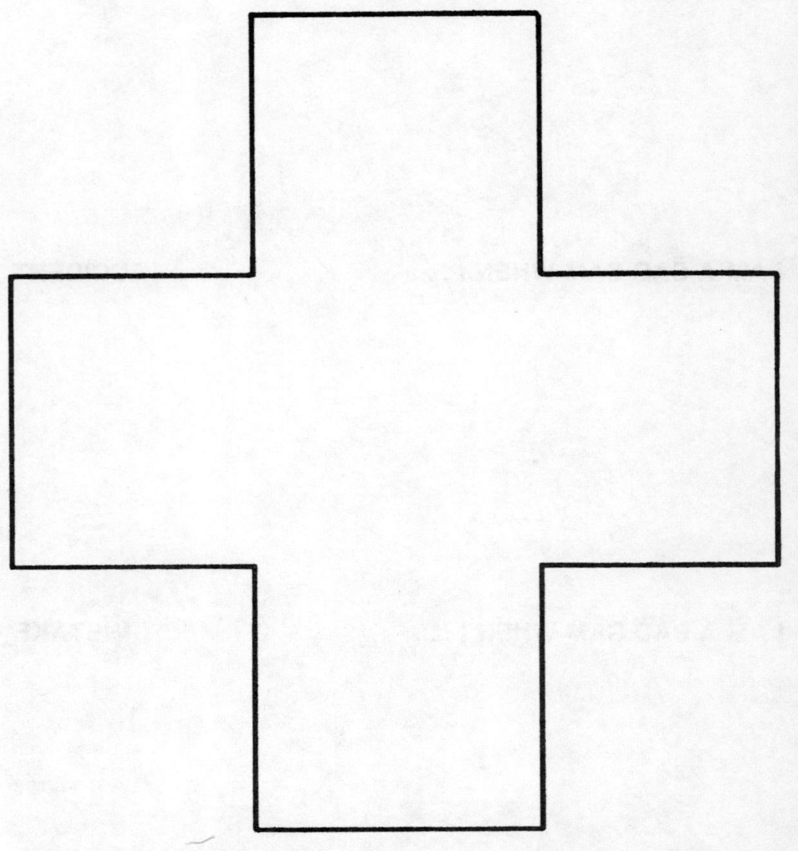

Pattern 6
Lesson 8

I MAKE PEOPLE SAD BY

I MAKE PEOPLE HAPPY BY

Pattern 7
Lesson 9

EXAMINATION OF CONSCIENCE QUESTIONS

Do I pray every day?

Do I go to Mass every Sunday (or Saturday evening)?

Do I say God's name with love?

Do I listen to my parents? Do I obey them?

Do I share with my brothers and sisters? With others?

Do I behave in class?

Do I tell the truth?

Do I take good care of my body?

Do I do my best in school? At home?

Pattern 8
Lesson 9

FAMILY PROMISE PAPER

THE ____ FAMILY

PROMISES TO BE MORE LOVING AS A FAMILY BY

SIGNED (Each family member puts their name on this paper)

____

____

____

____

____

____

Pattern 9
Lesson 10

FATHER GIVES ME ABSOLUTION.

WE MAY READ THE WORD OF GOD.

FATHER WELCOMES ME.

I PRAY AN ACT OF CONTRITION.

I CONFESS MY SINS.

FATHER AND I GIVE THANKS.

FATHER GIVES ME A PENANCE.